MW00453687

Famous & Fun Classics
14 Appealing Piano Arrangements
Carol Matz

Famous & Fun Classics, Book 4, is a wonderful introduction to the timeless masterworks of the great composers. The collection includes arrangements of themes from symphonic, operatic and keyboard literature, carefully selected for their appeal to students. These early-intermediate arrangements can be used as a supplement to any method. Book 4 introduces $\frac{6}{8}$ time, and features arrangements in the keys of C, G and D major, as well as A minor and E minor. At the end of the book, you will find pages "About the Composers," which contain interesting biographical information in language that is easy to understand. Enjoy your experience with these musical masterpieces.

Carol Matz

Andaluza (No. 5 from *Twelve Spanish Dances*) 28
Barber of Seville, The (Overture) 16
Can-Can (from the operetta *Orpheus in the Underworld*) 2
Eine Kleine Nachtmusik 20
Gymnopédie I 18
Hungarian Dance, No. 5 (Brahms) 12
"Italian" Symphony, Theme from the 26
March of the Toreadors (from the opera *Carmen*) 4
March Slav 5
O mio babbino caro (from the opera *Gianni Schicchi*) 24
Polovetsian Dance (from the opera *Prince Igor*) 14
Swan Lake, Theme from 8
Symphony No. 9, *From the New World* 6
Waltz, Op. 39, No. 15 (Brahms) 10
About the Composers 30

Can-Can

(from the operetta *Orpheus in the Underworld*)

Jacques Offenbach (1819–1880)
Arr. by Carol Matz

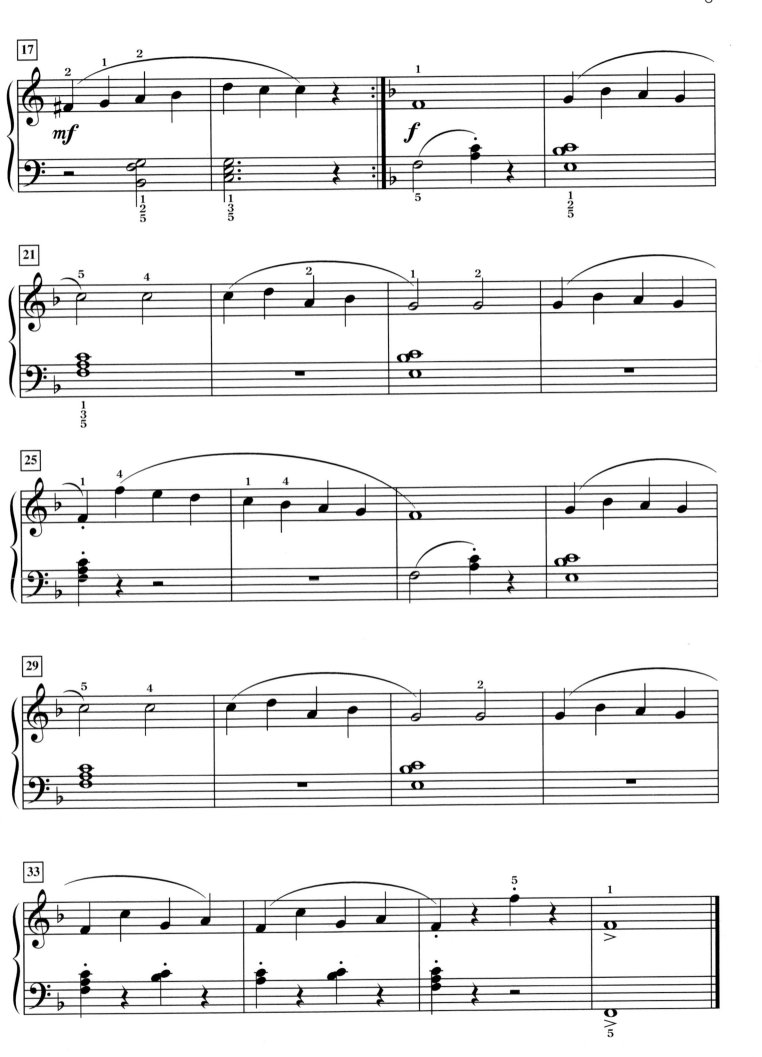

March of the Toreadors

(from the opera *Carmen*)

Georges Bizet (1838–1875)
Arr. by Carol Matz

With excitement

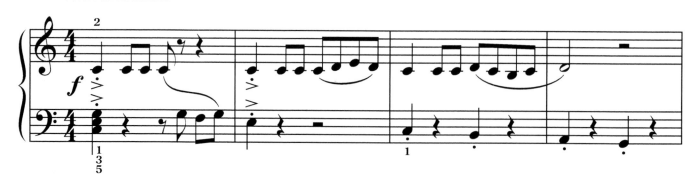

March Slav

Peter Ilyich Tchaikovsky (1840–1893)
Arr. by Carol Matz

Symphony No. 9, "From the New World"

(Second Movement)

Antonín Dvořák (1841–1904)
Arr. by Carol Matz

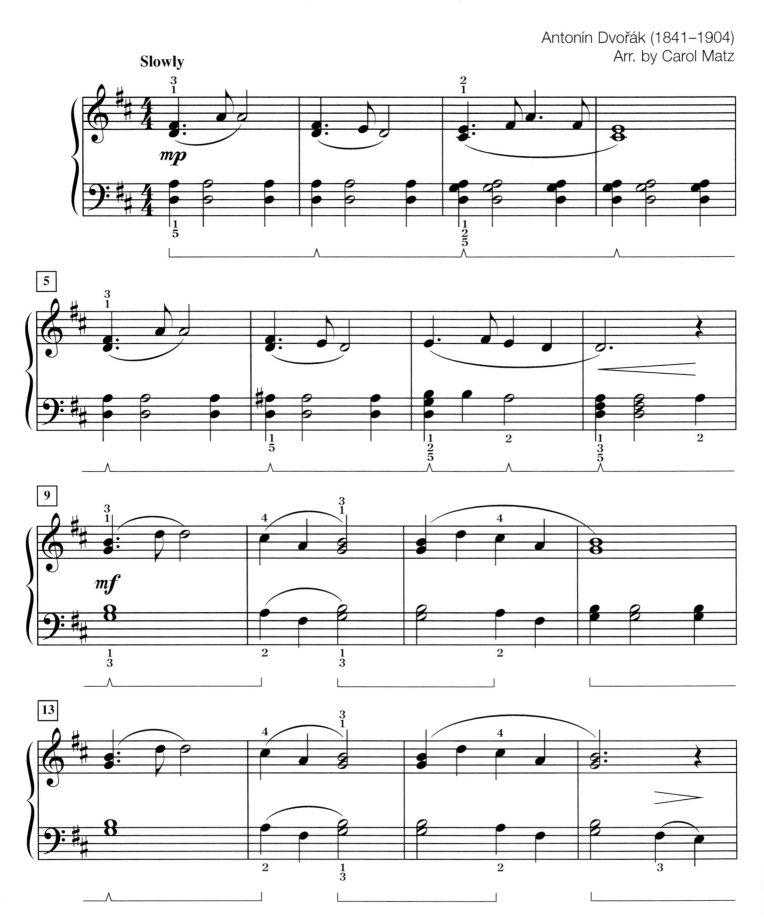

Theme from
Swan Lake

Peter Ilyich Tchaikovsky (1840–1893)
Arr. by Carol Matz

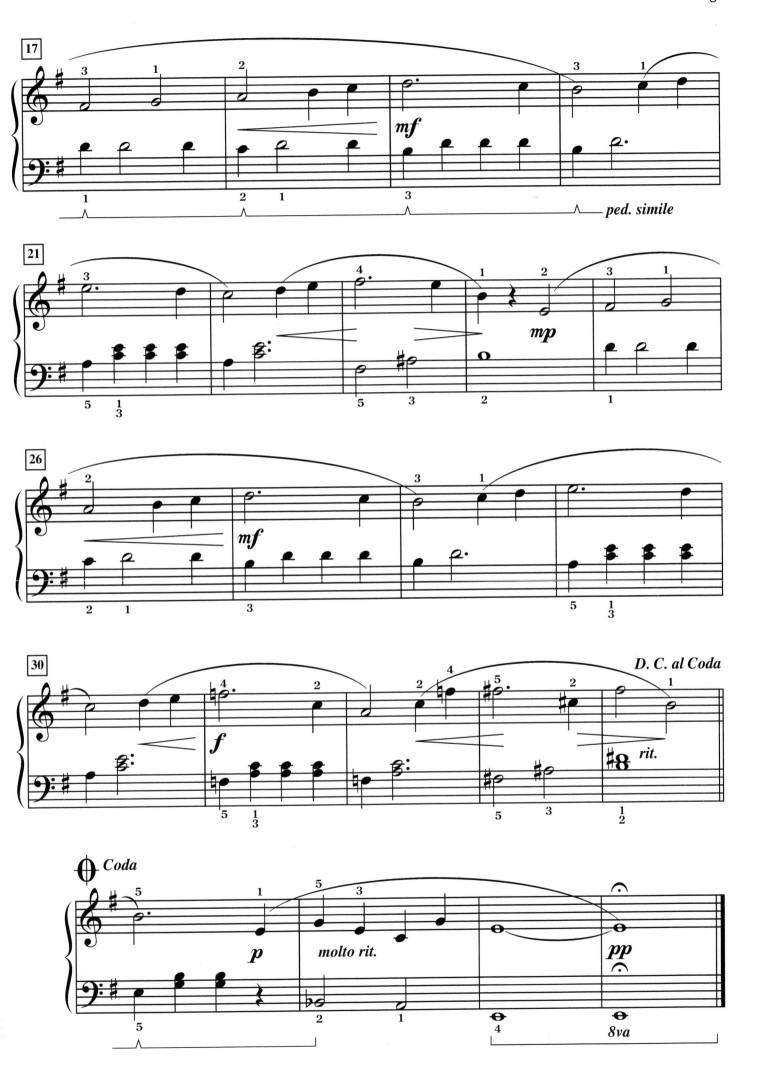

Waltz
(Op. 39, No. 15)

Johannes Brahms (1833–1897)
Arr. by Carol Matz

Tenderly

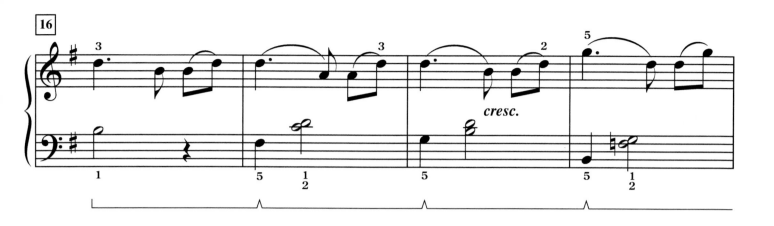

Hungarian Dance
(No. 5)

Johannes Brahms (1833–1897)
Arr. by Carol Matz

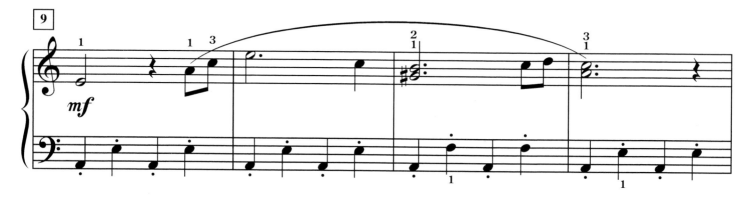

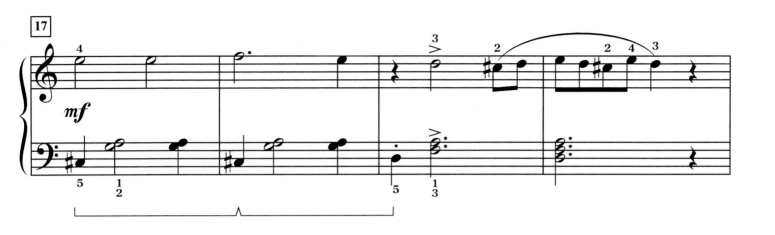

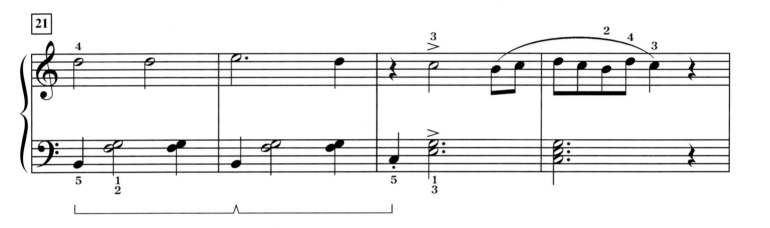

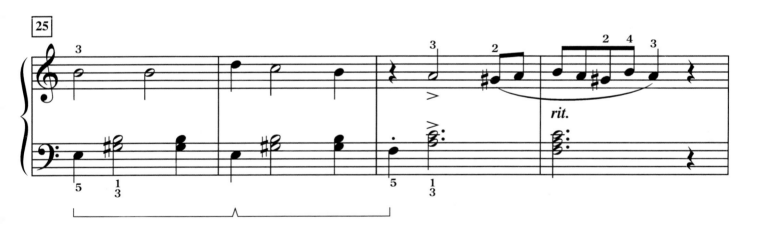

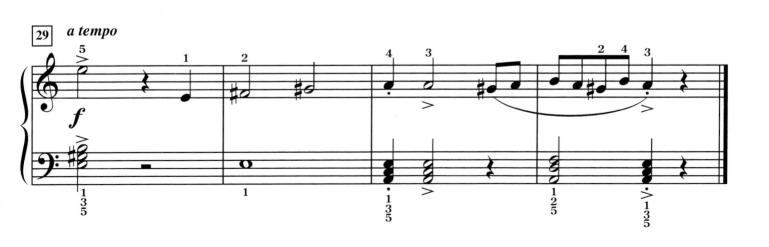

Polovetsian Dance

(from the opera *Prince Igor*)

Alexander Borodin (1833–1887)
Arr. by Carol Matz

Overture to
The Barber of Seville

Gioachino Rossini (1792–1868)
Arr. by Carol Matz

Gymnopédie I

Erik Satie (1866–1925)
Arr. by Carol Matz

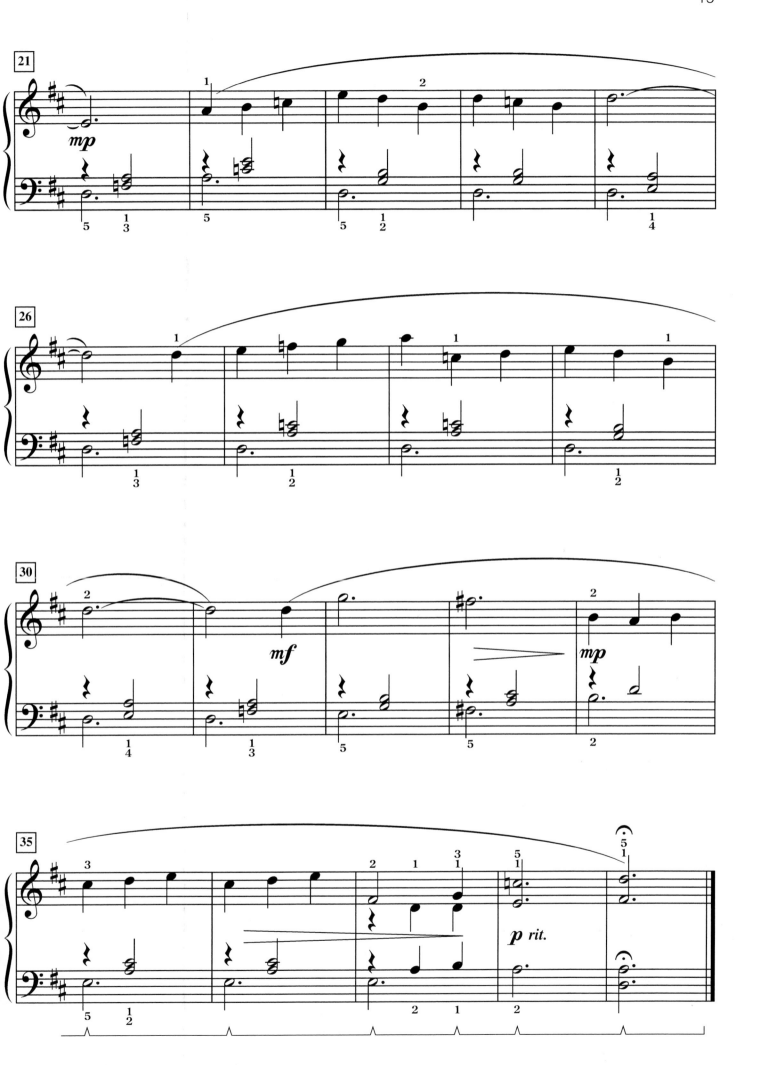

Eine Kleine Nachtmusik
(A Little Night Music)

(First Movement)

Wolfgang Amadeus Mozart (1756–1791)
Arr. by Carol Matz

Fast

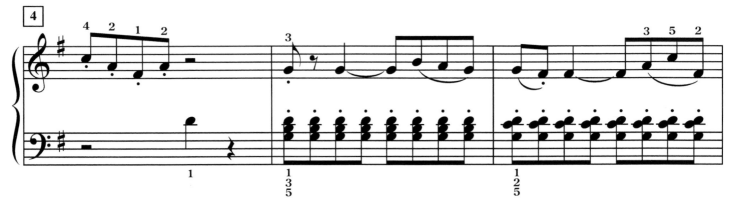

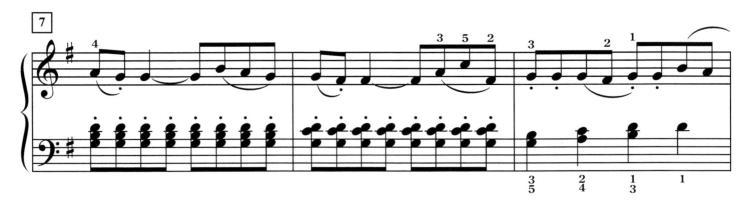

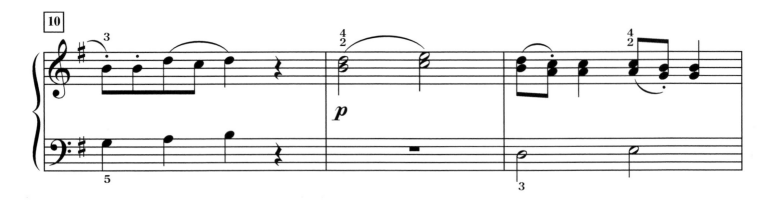

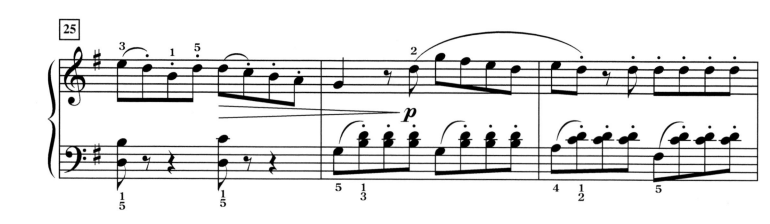

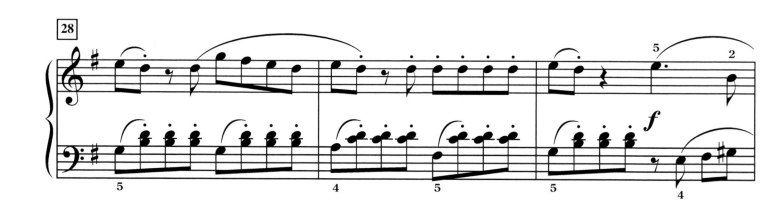

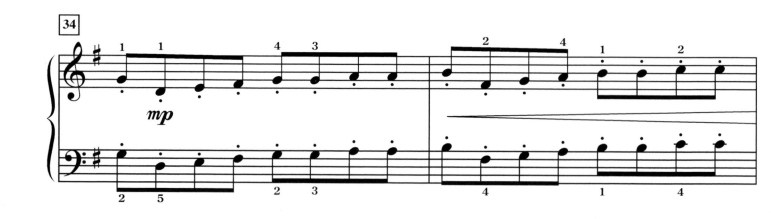

O mio babbino caro
(Oh, My Dear Father)
(from the opera *Gianni Schicchi*)

Giacomo Puccini (1858–1924)
Arr. by Carol Matz

Theme from the
"Italian" Symphony

(Symphony No. 4)

Felix Mendelssohn (1809–1847)
Arr. by Carol Matz

Andaluza

(No. 5 from *Twelve Spanish Dances*)

Enrique Granados (1867–1916)
Arr. by Carol Matz

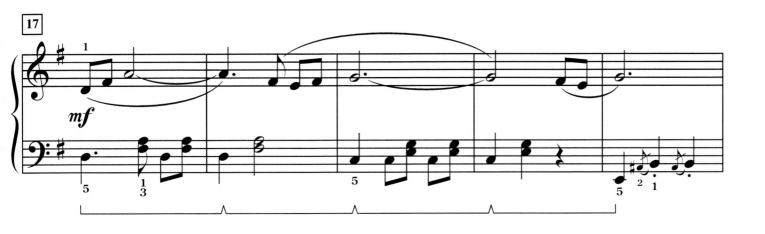

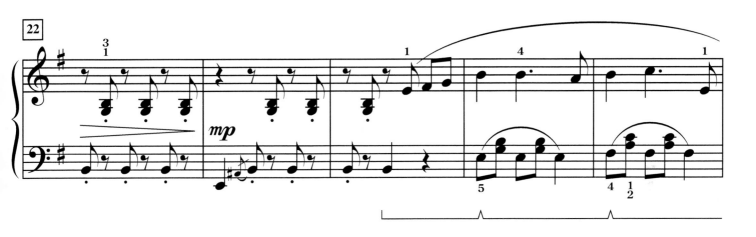

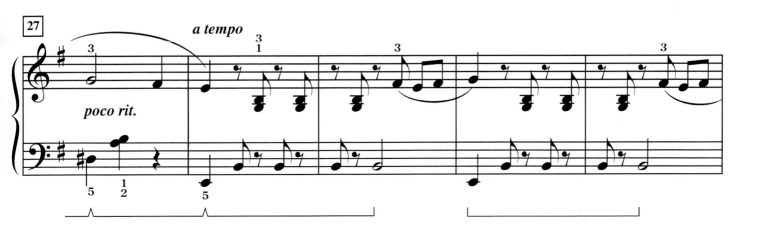

About the Composers

Georges Bizet
Born October 25, 1838; died June 3, 1875
Nationality: French

Both of Bizet's parents were musicians. His father gave Georges his first music lessons at the age of four. Bizet became an accomplished pianist, and went on to study composition. In his lifetime, he wrote over 150 piano pieces, a symphony, operas and other works. His masterpiece, the opera *Carmen,* is performed throughout the world.

Alexander Borodin
Born November 12, 1833; died February 27, 1887
Nationality: Russian

Alexander Borodin was brilliant at a young age. By the time he was a teenager, he could speak four languages, as well as play the piano, cello and flute. He eventually became a medical doctor and a professor of chemistry, and composed music as a hobby. His greatest work is the opera *Prince Igor*, which was unfinished when he died. Two fellow composers later completed the opera so that it could be performed.

Johannes Brahms
Born May 7, 1833; died April 3, 1897
Nationality: German

Brahms grew up in a very poor neighborhood. As a young man, he played the piano in dance halls to help support his family. He eventually became such a successful composer that he never had to take other jobs to earn a living. Brahms was quite absent-minded; legend has it that he often forgot to attach his suspenders and almost lost his pants many times while conducting!

Antonín Dvořák
Born September 8, 1841; died May 1, 1904
Nationality: Czech

Dvořák grew up in a small village in the country, with six brothers and sisters. He eventually left to study music and became a prize-winning composer. Later in his life, he traveled to America where he wrote his symphony *From the New World.* Next to music, Dvořák's biggest passion was trains, and he often visited railway stations to watch them.

Enrique Granados
Born July 27, 1867; died March 24, 1916
Nationality: Spanish

Granados began piano lessons when he was 12, and started studying composition a few years later. At the age of 22, he published his *Twelve Spanish Dances*, which made him internationally famous. Many years later, Granados sailed to the United States for the premiere of his opera and to perform at the White House. Sadly, on his return trip, his ship was torpedoed by a German submarine and both Granados and his wife drowned.

Felix Mendelssohn
Born February 3, 1809; died November 4, 1847
Nationality: German

Mendelssohn's parents encouraged him to be a musician. The family regularly held afternoon concerts at their house, so Mendelssohn was surrounded by music at an early age. By the time he was a teenager, Mendelssohn had already written some of his greatest pieces.

Wolfgang Amadeus Mozart
Born January 27, 1756; died December 5, 1791
Nationality: Austrian

By the time he was six years old, Mozart was an outstanding pianist, performing all across Europe. He composed his first piece of music when he was four, and wrote his first opera when he was twelve. Mozart wrote a huge amount of music and became a world-famous composer. Unfortunately, he died when he was only 35 years old.

Jacques Offenbach
Born June 20, 1819; died October 5, 1880
Nationality: German-born, lived in France

As a boy living in Germany, Offenbach was a wonderful cellist who gave public concerts. His father, a synagogue cantor, sent him to study cello in Paris, since he felt that Jews had more opportunities in France than in Germany. Offenbach became a successful theater conductor in France and composed about 90 operettas.

Giacomo Puccini
Born December 22, 1858; died November 29, 1924
Nationality: Italian

For generations, Puccini's family worked as church composers and organists. At first, he followed their example by working in the church, but one night he walked 13 miles to see Verdi's opera *Aida*, and he realized his true passion was opera. He went on to become one of the greatest opera composers of all time.

(continued)

About the Composers (continued)

Gioachino Rossini

Born February 29, 1792; died November 13, 1868
Nationality: Italian

Rossini was exposed to music by his parents (his mother
was an opera singer and his father played the trumpet).
Rossini learned to play piano and sing, and wrote his first
opera when he was only 18. He sometimes wrote as many
as three or four operas a year!

Erik Satie

Born May 17, 1866; died July 1, 1925
Nationality: French

As a young man, Satie studied music at the Paris
Conservatory. However, his real passion was playing piano
in the Parisian cafés. Satie became known for his absurd
sense of humor. Many of his pieces have very silly titles,
such as *Three Real Flabby Preludes for a Dog* and *Being
Jealous of His Friend with the Big Head*. The French
composers Debussy and Ravel were among his friends.

Peter Ilyich Tchaikovsky

Born May 7, 1840; died November 6, 1893
Nationality: Russian

Although Tchaikovsky began studying music as a young boy,
he ended up going to law school and getting a job with the
government. However, Tchaikovsky never lost his love of
music and he eventually taught and composed music for a
living. In 1891, he traveled to New York to conduct his music
at the opening of the famous Carnegie Hall.